CSU Poetry Series XXVIII

Jeanne Murray Walker

Coming into History

Cleveland State University Poetry Center

ACKNOWLEDGMENTS

Thanks to the following periodicals for permission to reprint some of these poems:

2 PLUS 2: "Giving Up the Sofa," "While the Men Are Gone"

THE AMERICAN VOICE: "How Labor Starts"

BOULEVARD: "Carpenter Sets His Own House on Fire"

THE GEORGIA REVIEW: "Parkers Prairie, Minnesota"

IRIS: "Reading *The New York Times*," "Sleep," "Thinking about My Own Death"

NIMROD: "February," "My Grandmother Called Me by Everything but My Own Name"

NORTHWEST REVIEW: "Nursing"

PAINTED BRIDE QUARTERLY: "The Child Molester"

PARTISAN REVIEW: "Recovering the Commonplace"

PASSAGES NORTH: "The Bag of Stones," "Shirt"

POETRY: "Birth," "Flying Home," "I Won't Read the Alphabet Book Once More," "Inspecting the Garden After Dark," "Invocation to a Baby Already Twelve Days Overdue," "Seizure," "The Shawl," "Theater"

PRAIRIE SCHOONER: "American Tourist at Covent Garden," "Cold War," "Cutpurse," "Driving by Westminster Abbey After Midnight," "Driving Home in the Blizzard," "London Underground," "Paddington Station at Midnight." Reprinted from PRAIRIE SCHOONER by permission of University of Nebraska Press. Copyright 1988, University of Nebraska Press.

SHENANDOAH: "Blind Genius Discovers Infinity," "Meteoroid Falls in Farmer's Back Yard"

WESTBRANCH: "Man's Thumb Bleeds for Three Years," "Man Survives Nine Days in Rubble of Collapsed Bakery," "Sweethearts Vanish in Tunnel of Love"

WHETSTONE: "Talking to the Baby after Teaching a Poetry Workshop"

I am grateful to the Pennsylvania Council on the Arts for a Fellowship and to The University of Delaware for a Leave of Absence which allowed me the time to complete this book.

The Women Writers' Group in Philadelphia has given me, for as long as this manuscript has been underway, generous and warm support. Deborah Burnham, Fleda Jackson, and E. Daniel Larkin were companions without whom the book could not have been written.

The series of poems set in London, which comprise the third section of this book, won The Prairie Schooner/Strousse Award for 1988.

Funded Through
Ohio Arts Council

727 East Main Street
Columbus, Ohio 43205-1796
(614) 466-2613

CONTENTS

For
Henrietta Juliann Kruse Aderhold
my grandmother
who never met Jack

THE SHAWL

Somewhere on Ellis Island
my mother's mother lost the shawl
the women of the town crocheted for her
out of mauves and purples,
old tunes twisted in the strands,
and clever plots
woven, woven in the pattern.
It was a gift.

Away from that shawl
my mother's mother had to move,
toward the waiting train, toward Minnesota,
through the smell of gasoline,
through the sycamores
whose leaves clinked down
like foreign coins.
She tripped over
a broken step, caught herself,

steadied her canvas bag, paid
her money, wrote her name on the form, washed
in communal showers, put on
her skirt with its stubborn hem. When
they opened the wire gate, she bowed
and hoisted the bag higher
to step over the threshold
into the calling distance
where the years stretched out
plain as good dirt

and she began to imagine
the calamity and extreme grace
of someone wearing that mauve shawl
till every night in dreams
she chopped it,
burned it, and
when it rose again,
she buried it.

She spent every minute
chasing the furious rooster, dropping
report cards into her apron pocket, bargaining
in zero weather,
forgetting that old grace,
finally carrying
her children's
children on her hip,
while she stirred the soup,

their breath soft as moss,
their tiny feet
stuttering against her.
My feet, my breath.
She bore my mother
like a speck toward me
as I bear you
in this plain dress
towards your own children,
holding in my empty hands
her glorious shawl,
sunrise over Ellis Island.

NURSING

Waiting for the milk to come, you hold so still
that I imagine you years from now, maybe
when I am dead and you are an old man
anchored in some boat on Lake Miltona
deep in reeds, late in Fall, the water
so cold it hardly remembers its own name,
you think the shapes of fish, calling them
from sleep: sunfish, walleye pike, muskie,
the way my father called the stars at night
leaning in his jacket on the railing
till out of darkness fire spun to us
while we held still: Big Dipper, Little Dipper,
Orion, and the tall North Star. He didn't
reel them hand over hand. He only thought
their names into the unimaginable darkness
the way I lie still here beside you and
your children come, calling their own children
from the place further and further away
where everything is stunned by grace to silence.
And then, all of a sudden, the milk comes.

PARKERS PRAIRIE, MINNESOTA

Bloomquist's Hardware burned its lights
in the bad part of town when the bad part
was three blocks long and bad meant hoboes
hunched there, feeding their cold fires.
If you'll let me, I can put you on that street,
beside my father. Hold his hand,
step over the wooden doorsill.

His rough hunting jacket may brush your cheek.
Maybe you feel like crying because
you don't know him, Jack, your namesake, as he hollers
"Hank! You have two-inch finishing nails?"

Can you see Hank Bloomquist in the far dark
of the old store hitch up his pants? He calls
"You bet." Three hundred fifty pounds of farmer,
gone soft because of a bum leg, limps toward you
over the rough seas of warped board floor

while your grandfather spreads his hands
to the wood-burning stove, the fire flashing
on his teeth, on his fox-colored hair.

He starts to talk his stories, about some guy
whose lonely life is out of kilter,
who needs to fix everything he owns, even
the Lala Ka Trigger of the Come and Go Rod.

He runs his fingers through a keg of nails
to get the bad ones out. He is still healthy
and it's nineteen fifty-two.
                              Sit on the floor
and watch the moon rise through the window like a relic.
Even in the bad part of town, I don't believe
you'll come to any harm if you spread your hands,
like he does, towards the stories.

THE BAG OF STONES

Winters, I wake up partly to forget the story
a friend handed me when it got too heavy,
a bag of stones I'll have to carry till I die.
Sometimes I would do anything to relieve its weight.
Watch me open my bag to lighten it.
Don't read. Don't read.

It's Viet Nam. 1970. A hut outside of town.
The father's walked to town to buy supplies
and won't be back till nightfall.
In weak November sun, the mother hangs up wash.
Twin babies crawl beneath brush
and several children forage for dead wood
where pines breathe, at the edge of the clearing.
A dark child whittles clothespins.
He doesn't see the Marines creeping toward him.
They have him tied before he feels their hands.
And Nama, the oldest—they thong her to a pole
and start a fire.
     The mother hurries
the others inside, bolts the doors, shutters
the windows, piles chairs, heaves tables—

"Come out," the white men call. Their voices
walk in boots. They'll let go
if everyone comes out. But the mother counts
her children. She has to save the three she can.
Flames fold Nama, blackening, into them. Watching
between boards, the mother weeps. She weeps
and weeps. Then Sim runs weeping,

bleeding toward his mother's door. He pounds.
Let me in! he screams. She slumps
against the latch, head swimming.
      That's when
I invent the door that stays open while it's closed,

the fire that burns everything but children.
That's when I pretend on both sides of the door
they realize they're holding pieces
of the same puzzle and it's the face of God.
That's when I pretend you can end a story
any way you want to.

SEIZURE

for Howard Rabinowitz, Jack's doctor

I gave you what I could when you were born,
salt water to rock you,
your half of nine month's meat,
miles of finished veins,
and all the blood I had to spare.

And then I said, this is the last time
I divide myself in half, the last time
I lie down in danger and rise bereft,
the last time I give up half my blood.

Fifteen months later, when I walked into your room
your mobile of the sun, moon,
and stars was tilting
while your lips twisted,
while you arched your back.

Your fingers groped for something in the air.
Your arms and legs flailed like broken wings.
Your breath was a load too heavy
for your throat to heave into your lungs.
You beat yourself into a daze against your crib.
We slapped your feet,
we flared the lights,
we doused you in a tub of lukewarm water.
But your black eyes rolled.
You had gone somewhere
and left behind a shape of bluish skin,
a counterfeit of you.
                        It was then,
before the red wail of the police car,
before the IV's, before the medicine
dripped into you like angels, before you woke
to a clear brow, to your own funny rising voice,

it was then I would have struck the bargain,
all my blood for your small shaking.
I would have called us even.

SHOWING MY SON A PICTURE
OF MY BROTHER AT A HAM RADIO

Why are his lips so thin?
He was sick, that's why.
What is he doing?
He is constructing the world
from noise and longing.

    Oh brother, adjusting the headset
    over blond curls the color
    of pencil shavings,
    sitting in front of that
    black box, twirling a dial.

Does he look like anyone?
Like one thin fisherman before him,
an uncle's cousin, who turned
sideways to the sea in Sweden
and slipped inside the wind.

    He is listening for
    some frequency, some flash,
    some language
    beyond the periphery: Spanish,
    maybe, or Japanese.

And who looks like him?
At night, deer, staring into headlights
and in the daytime, you,
looking at this picture in my lap,
kicking your sandals against my thigh.

    Oh brother, the genius
    in black and white
    who strung wires, heard voices
    in the headset only he
    could understand.

Did he die?
So young he never had a son.
He never met a person who
spoke Spanish, never
saw this picture.

    He watched his little sister,
    running healthy rings around him,
    laughing so she couldn't hear
    any truth in all
    that static.

Who took this picture?
I did, his little sister,
standing in his doorway, wanting
to say "I only speak plain English.
Come in. Come in,"

    while he kept casting
    his voice into the night
    like a lonely net.
    Ask me what I've learned
    since then.

I have learned Death
is a tall interpreter and
you are another language
your uncle speaks in,
your blond curls, so near
I finally understand.

FEBRUARY

I am walking down Hamilton Street at dusk
to pick up my youngest child at my friend's house,
during a winter of cruel weather,
every step dragging me further into the old dark.
The sky is pressing down like pot lid,

the icy wind whips like a slave driver.
We must have done something terrible against nature
because the hedges claw at my skirt,
and the stink of rotting leaves drifts into
all my openings until I think of death, of death.

We have banded together against cold wind,
we have cooked one another soup from roots,
we have gathered our children into lit corners
of living rooms and made up brave stories,
told stories of hopscotch someday in impossible sunlight

but this time, winter may stay forever.
It is the exact moment when pitch darkness is pouring
into the milky twilight of late afternoon
and the smell of damp wool rises from my jacket.
I am plodding by mounds of filthy snow.

But the brutal street for once is holding its breath,
the cars pinned to a stoplight at the corner,
and I feel warmth lay its hand on my shoulder.
The wind, after sobbing for weeks, catches its breath
and I can see the clouds part to a clear shining.

By chance I glance between two houses,
I am allowed to see for one pure moment
how over night the light can fly back home
and be singing in the branches by next morning,
how all the stories we tell our children are true.

MY GRANDMOTHER CALLED ME BY
EVERYTHING BUT MY OWN NAME

When I think of the way my grandmother, calling me,
would sort through names of the living and the dead,
her voice settling briefly on each child—
Gretta, Samuel, Joseph, Sophie, Alice—
before it perched and nested in my name,

it makes me think of all the surplus names
in other houses from Tacoma to New York.
They could be fluttering beside your windows.
They might be flapping in your fireplace flues,
some of them stuck under dirty kitchen tile.

I want to save the names of all our kin.
I want them to come pouring down for us
from family trees like loads of bright fall apples
into a sheet so we can gather its corners
and bring them home where they can feed us.

I want us to carry one or two in our pockets
for courage when we go into strange neighborhoods
where thieves wait under amber streetlights.
I want us to send names up for flares
when we sit in a dark lonely house,

because my father's name is the name of your uncle
and the history they dug out of the earth together
is like the complicated tunnels of the subway
where every track connects with every other.
Maybe soon none of us will be far from the names.

Then no U-Haul, not even the American Van Lines
will be able to take you far enough from home
so you forget Aunt Hilda, face powder trapped in wrinkles,
her eyes like racoon eyes, her little kind hands
pressing a chocolate into your warm palm.

WHILE THE MEN ARE GONE

All over Powelton Village women are conceiving children
as though these were the last days before the Second Coming.
Sally Hammerman stands on the red brick walk beside
her fat twin, Rosie, & her thin twin, Phanny, reciting
the names of pregnant women, like a psalm

to destroy death. At Thirty-fifth & Baring,
someone's blond daughter waits for the bus, her stomach
lifting her flowered dress toward a second chance.
Before the bus can sigh & let her on, a woman raises
a 2nd storey window & cries for joy that she has conceived.

Nursling chrysanthemums on Marilyn Taylor's porch
open their purple eyes & praise the light.
We are all stocking children for nine months' delivery.
We are reveling in new bodies, we are filling
& emptying diaper pails, we are wiping noses,

we are never finishing our sentences, we are flying
apart, faces here, names there, occupation,
age, address—our souls & bodies spinning quietly to pieces,
whirling closer & closer to the final light,
because this is the four horsemen & the four beasts

& the four & twenty elders gathered around the sun.
Because the angel of birth has come to put one foot
on City Hall, & one foot on the Wissahickon
& one foot on Baring Street.

THE CARS ON WALNUT STREET STOP
TO LET A DOG CROSS

The driver squints, sees the dog, and hits
his brakes, checking his rear view mirror to discover
cars filling Walnut Street like a spreading stain.
Think of all that metal idling while drivers watch,

the way ushers might watch a rich patron sink into
his seat and sleep, because right now the Irish Setter
has decided to nap in the middle of Walnut Street,
so he points his bottom toward heaven and arches his body,

inches his paws forward till he's flat
as a shadow and the cars kneel before him, headlights
flicking on here and there, like an audience
putting opera glasses up. Someone in the back row

decides to play his horn, which makes the setter
want to get up and dance, zigzagging from curb
to curb, whirling his raggy tail until
drivers climb out, slam their doors like applause

and ascend their hoods for a better view while the dog
begins waltzing on two legs with a beautiful lady driver
in a pin-stripe suit, and the audience forgets dinner
to hurl parking tickets and shopping lists like confetti

because this is the hour of the dog in Philadelphia.
This is the day Chrysler and Toyota and Ford
canceled their business to save a fleeting heart
and Walnut Street is the place of the cherubim.

EVOLUTION: PHILADELPHIA ZOO, AUGUST, 1987

So much is already over for the tortoise.
On the day we visit the zoo in crucifying heat,
he is a huge, dirty heart, all of his tires gone flat.
In the beginning the animals must have had equal chances.

Think of the tiger practicing cunning while glaciers melted,
and the monkey tricking his way to questionable grace.
But the tortoise must have fumbled without a plan,
no engine of ambition throbbing under his hump,

no candle lighting the chambers of his brain,
and now look, he's a ruin in the dust. But no matter,
the zookeeper unlocks the gate and enters his yard
wearing her decent plain face and her coveralls,

dragging a hose to fill his small lake.
Even in the terrible heat, she is so serene
she might be a woman stepping into a bus
or handing a street vendor nickels for an orange,

and the tortoise slowly puts out his leathery head,
blinking his bald eyes. He can hardly believe
his luck. Trying to recall which leg to move first,
he starts out to greet her, full of clumsy joy.

When he finally reaches her, he butts his nose
against her thick thigh. She scratches his prehistoric
neck with her human fingers. There is no love
like theirs. Any minute they might begin

to sing. Any minute they might fly out of
their bodies like bright newfangled animals,
showing how veins and livers and skeletons
can be perfected for something we never thought of.

I WON'T READ THE ALPHABET BOOK ONCE MORE

I can't look at A for Aging
or B for Bored and Broken Down
or C for Clock. All afternoon
the H has been doing the same job,
standing on this page like
a hippopotamus, holding
the heavy purple sky on his back.

Why can't the sky invent new legs
to prop beneath its storm clouds
so the H can finally walk off the page?
How can I go on allowing the M
to be made into a monkey
over and over without any pity?
There is going to be a revolution.

I can feel the band strike up
in my blood. In my chest
I can feel the bullets flying.
You shout *Read! Read! Read!*
but my shoulders are already hoisting
themselves like two flags,
fluttering away from here.

Under the circumstances,
I pull your stroller down,
and take you to the zoo. There
the sky floats effortlessly.
There the hippo loves his body
merely because it holds him down to earth.
See how he raises his mouth

easily into the vast purple air,
teeth scarred as ancient bricks?
He is letting his leathery tongue ride out,
unhinging the shovels of his jaw,

rolling the sun in his mouth
like a wild cry of joy.
It is the fiery letter Oh!

The hippo cures the alphabet.
We can live in the same house
with that book again.
We can take back all the letters—
mean-spirited X, boisterous R,
even the overworked, weeping H.
I push your stroller home. Hopeful.
Hurdy gurdy. Hindsight. Hallelujah.

STORY PROBLEM

At midnight in her apartment Patsy can hear moss
growing like grief outside her window and the cars

on the Parkway whispering, loss, loss.
From center city Philadelphia, she can hear

Roy counting stars in Cleveland. At what rate
would Patsy drive if she leaves Philadelphia at eight

and gets to Cleveland in ten hours, given that six
black sheep bleat across the road just south

of Carlisle and that she has to diagnose and fix
the carburetor of her ailing Plymouth,

that a hose fills and empties the swimming pool
in Akron at 16 dozen gallons per hour on Thursday but

lags on holidays and when the weather's cool,
and thinking of this, she's unable to shut

her glove compartment, where maps jumble and spill,
maps that possibly could save her miles

or send her down roads where nobody kills
anyone else. And calculate that some waitress smiles

in a highway restaurant and that in Cleveland somewhere
a housewife buys five steaks at three bucks a pound

and grills two of them with garlic. To be fair,
it must be said the wind is blowing. The ground

is slightly wet. The papers are a mess
at the table where you're working. Your stress

will affect the answer, which must be precise
to the hundred millionth place. Roy slumps

in his cold and empty bed. Can you see his eyes?
Patsy must get there, regardless, regardless.

GIVING UP THE SOFA

That sofa was just cotton batting
and fabric with red-eyed peacocks walking in it,
but the day it was delivered you called me
to marvel at how its weave drank up your light.

That day we celebrated till it seemed safely yours.
By nightfall you had installed its peacocks
in your wisdom. But Hearne's didn't care.
What does money know? That's why, four months later,
I had to cross 34th again to mourn with you
while two boys, shy to your daughter's tears,
hoisted the peacocks out of light and took your sofa back.

Nothing made for sitting on, nothing
that can be repossessed, could cause such flagrant sorrow.
Sofa must have been the word for something else.
Getting over it is like getting over death,
like catching light which, Look! still falls
on your daughter's shoulders as she sits on the floor.

From now on, where the sofa was there will be air.
But here's your daughter, her lovely collar bone,
the hollow all the world's best things
won't ever fill and here's how sunshine
floods it easily. Could it be
that when they took your sofa what remained
was so pure it made our hearts pulse in our throats,
so blank we really saw each other,
so final that for a moment we could feel
the speed of light.

TALKING TO THE BABY AFTER TEACHING
A POETRY WORKSHOP

This is what I said to them: a poem's
a fireworks of love and misery.
Sofas, houses, cars—things that can be
repossessed, actual things—forget them.

Then driving home, my old fear returned,
You could be repossessed, dead in the Spring,
your insistent mouth gone from my breast,
your cries packed up like bright nickels
growing dull with time and nothing under
heaven to remind us how your skin
smelled, not mint, not sage, not roses, nothing.

You probably won't die. But even if you live
you'll be so real you'll scare us, the way
you scatter sparks like fireworks, *thing, thing,*
thing, your applesauce against the walls,
your blocks and diapers littering the rooms
more scandalously real than a sofa.

And you are leering at me, your round face
actual as the old sun, as though to taunt
Write a poem which doesn't have things in it,
a poem all shadowy and vacant. Go on. Write it.

POEM IN LIEU OF VEGETABLES

While we were standing by the corn in Acme,
peeling back husks to see the kernels
rising like new moons,
she found you in the grocery cart again.
You were stretching out your hands
towards worlds of curly broccoli,
towards a new shore of carrots.

She bent the way she always does
and whispered the old words
I'm hungry. There's not enough,
trudging down the aisle,
her little feet wrapped up in plastic bags,
her fingers picking at the knot

of her transparent rain hat,
the same old angry stye, the same
brown lips moving in a mixed-up song.
That's when fear sweeps through the city
like a summer thunder storm.
That's when the lights flicker,

that's when the cash register starts
clicking like a loaded gun.

RESPONSIBLE CHOICE

Just before dawn she visits babies.
She walks between brick buildings,
by the unshaven Italian selling newspapers,
who winks like the morning star.
When she opens the door, the babies stand and cheer.
The baby with the cleft in his chin smiles.
The baby with one blue and one brown eye
recites the alphabet.
Another baby looks up from building a whole city
and sings. She checks her coin purse.
Oh Take Us Oh Take Us
the babies breathe in and out.
But she is poor and when she hears
morning scraping its forehead on the tall roofs
she wakes up, turning the babies back
to stillness, shaking them into air,
letting them vanish. She,
who would know how to love
the future, either way.

THE CHILD MOLESTER

*The sins of the fathers
are visited upon the children.*

On some day when ordinary light
washes the maples,
his tires may punish the gravel
beside your chain link fence,
beside the lilacs of your playlot.
I imagine that he'll snap off the key
and sit in his red and black plaid jacket,
his soft wrists dangling
over his jackknifed legs
and wait for you,
his lips parted by sunlight,
his green eyes darting like
little lizards over the foliage.
His face will be a hungry screen
where the same movie flickers
over and over: the heel
of his father's combat boots
expertly lowered on his fingers,
grinding, grinding.
He will move his scarred hands
to crack the window open
so breezes can lick his long sorrow.
I stand at a mother's distance,
watching spring return
to the playlot where lilacs break apart
to scatter, confetti on the wind.
I take your hand in this bad dream.
But I can't help you.
It will be exactly when
his thirty-one years slacken and fly apart
like birdshot, he will
find you, floating down the slide.
He will open his car door.
He will haul out his numb legs.
Then how can anyone stop him
from walking in the same old boots across
the green, innocent, defiled, unchanging grass?

FAIRY TALES

It's early April. Molly and I match
stories about you. Her fingers lengthen.
Light splatters down on her through the birch leaves
in our back yard just after her eleventh birthday.
She arches her wrist and sips her lemonade,
her straight hair straying from her pony tail
like pick-up sticks. She says she wants your hair
to look like hers. Straight. Blond.
As though you had one father. I say it doesn't matter.

But she's still trying to work the fractions:
half brother, half sister. Light crouches before her
like a supple cat. Her cat, Petunia, gathers paws
to leap into her lap. She buries her hands
in the cat's fiery, speckled fur, washes
her hands in sunlight. I would like to lie,
to say the light has answered all her questions.

But Unborn Stranger, you are perplexing
as light is to us both. Your shadow runs under
Molly's tongue like a blue vein, like a new lode
of wisdom. Thinking of you, we are women together.

LIGHT

All winter Molly sits like a disowned princess
in her broken kingdom, murmuring stories about you
as I do, stories which begin with the facts about
herself: that her father and I have been
divorced, that she teeters back and forth
between us, that half of her toys are here,
half there. For her, you are the toothless half
brother, pretender to her throne in all
her nightmares, the sign that her father's line
won't ever really rule. You are half
prince, half monster, who smirks and schemes to steal
the people's hearts while she looks on,
helpless as roses in the wallpaper.

But I tell her the true story. You'll grow and leave home.
One day a witch will come, blinking her blood-shot eye
to pluck you both from love. She'll stoke her fire,
cackling, her heart a dried-up pod. Together
you must shove her crooked shape into the oven
and steal together through darkness from bread crumb
to bread crumb all the way back home.

TALKING TO THE BABY ABOUT TAKING THE BUS

Dusk falls like a grudge early these days
and your blond sister, Molly, is miles away.
The world is wide with chance.
Someone has to teach her to survive the late bus
home from school, so I bundle you up
and drive to Germantown. All the way
the radio rotates like a motor at the center
of the world, spinning us on its dark axis:
rape murder robbery rape.

When we get there, Molly's oblivious,
an acrobat, she's Charlie Chaplin,
her arms and legs, flashing spokes.
She cartwheels down the lawn,
spinning above the snaggletoothed brick walks,
hand, foot, hand, practicing for balance.
She could be thrown off
by nothing, by the shadow of the
building on the sidewalk.

What can keep her safe against this
thinking dark on all her journeys home?
Nothing, the last light says,
but look. As I look
yards and yards of light descend, blushing
the stucco walls. The light is courteous.
It waits for the bus with us.

Sitting in your stroller, you laugh
and stretch your fingers toward the moon.
Molly dusts the earth from her palms.
Then she easily upends. She strides on her hands
across the sky and picks the moon up for you
with her toes. I have to close my eyes,
there is so much light.

STUDYING PHYSICS WITH MY DAUGHTER

For years now I have heard the cracking of
my memory, reluctantly falling apart like an
ancient building. At first a little cement dust,

then portions of the wall—The Natural Resources
Of Brazil, the Shape Of Utah—nothing,
in the beginning, that left me structurally unsound,

but it grew to a steady pouring—Co-efficients,
Participles, and Tammany Hall—lying in
the chilly basement of my mind mixed up together.

This went on for years, no matter how much
I paid bricklayers an hour, the slow habits of love
like shadows sliding across the yard each day,

and putting children to bed every night like
the relentless caress of wind on the foundation.
They wore me down to vague certainties.

That's why, when Molly came in her blue flannel
shirt and baggy jeans, holding her physics book,
I was surprised. I hardly recognized my child

rolling up her sleeves in the sharp daylight,
hauling enormous words into the sun
slapping them together with new mortar

so fast I could barely get the idea. Do you know,
she asks, why water climbs a paper napkin?
She says water and the napkin both have Partial Charges.

She says the word *Cohesion* and the word *Adhesion*.
Her words fall into the rubble in my poor memory.
I tell her I used to believe in physics.

But experience has taught me what makes water
climb a paper napkin. The water loves the napkin
and longs for it. My daughter turns her brilliant eyes

on me. She is the only teacher who can save me.
She goes to work, digging in the rubble.

II

BEAUTY QUEEN HAS MONSTER CHILD

She has vowed to reporters she
will keep the child. . . .

I've saved my beauty against the name they call you.
Monster. I gave up caring about beauty—as though
one day the rhinestone button on my coat
grew wobbly. One thread gave up and then
one more, until the button was hanging
off the coat. Finally, I ripped it free.

I can still feel beauty when I want to,
small and hard as a button in my pocket
underneath my finger tips. I'll give it to you.
May it be all the looks you'll ever need,
my face fixed in magazines and films—
the high cheekbones, gray eyes, the mole
above my lip, my skin as soft as cornsilk.

This beauty is like a mask that traps me.
I've struggled against it lately like a deer
who thrashes its eyes out in a hunter's snare,
or an opossum who will gnaw its leg off
to get free. But now, with you here,
your face off center, barely but terribly wrong,
I see how to escape.

I'll go with you as you make your way
from that fixed beauty, as the milky way
spins away from earth, like flock on flock
of buttons, cut loose together, spiraling upward,
opening out to everything imperfect, deep and
promising. I want to learn to spin away
from those old finished pictures of myself,
to wheel into the darkness where you are,
breathing further and further out, passing
winking stars that no astronomer
has thought of, till I get to the last,
brightest star, which is your face.

CARPENTER SETS HIS OWN HOUSE ON FIRE

                            About the house—
I built it with my father. It was an idea
we had together in a good season.
Later, I brought my wife and children there.
But as I grew older, it seemed too small,
like a story I had to tell my two sons
every day—the walls, the same old rooms.
I tried to rip it down, barehanded.
But father had dug the footings down to hell
and nailed the roof to the girders of the sky.
He'd tried to build it for all time, and while
it stood I couldn't think of how to build
another. I began to dream of fire.

It's a long story, and I'm not used to talking.
Most days, my hammer makes the noise for me.
Even my hammer stutters.

                            Well, one night,
I struck the match, stepped back to watch the fire,
then hurried to carry the kids out, one by one.
They slept that night beneath the strong trees
and felt the benediction of the clouds.
It was spring. The burning house
flickered in my sons' astonished eyes.
The fiery studs and beams against that night
was my new blueprint. I want to build again.
This plan is better than my father's.
It will keep out rain, I think, forever.

But they took my hammer and locked my tools away.
So who do you say I've hurt? The old house?
Surely not my father? The children?
They're sitting here before you, in this court.
Some people would call them beautiful.
This one could help to fix the crazy slope

of history with his sharp eye and one common
T square. The other's hands are subtle. I have
seen him plane rage until it's blunt and useful
as a walnut plank. They love me. They listen to me.
Look at them. If you let me go,
can you imagine what we might still finish?

METEOROID FALLS IN FARMER'S BACK YARD

Hold the check. No price you fellas quote me
will get you my quarter acre for your Park.
I'm writing to you—whoever gets this letter
at the Department of the Interior—to say
I could shave and put on my suit and drive
to Farmer's Mutual Bank today and have
the young Wilson kid withdraw enough to keep
me till I'm ninety. I don't believe in taking
from the State. Or giving to it, either.
I think a man should keep what is his own,
even if it's no good to him and the only thing
that he can do is stick it six feet under.

But what I wanted to say when I began—
I believe I saw this star when I was fourteen.
I grew up on this farm. I had a black pony
named King, and one August at sunset
my mother sent me for Virginia Slade,
the slow midwife down the road a ways.
My youngest sister was struggling to be born.
I didn't go back to gawk at women's business.
I swam, against the rules, in Johnson's pond,
where a broken stone slashed my left foot.
It bled like a stuck pig. I couldn't go home.
All night I lay in an alfalfa field,
smelling dust and greenness. I was naked.
Black, lumpy dirt clotted under my back
and the nettles scratched my forearms. But
what has stuck with me is that queer star,
how I had to squint a certain way
and lie on my side to get it. I thought
I'd seen a new star, that everything would change,
a clean sweep, that I would be important.
I was eating blueberries, sweet little worlds
one after another, till I was full and sleepy
as someone who had conquered everything.
After that I worked and planned and saved,

too crowded to inquire what star I'd seen.
But I carried it the way a girl would carry
a thorny white rose pressed in her pocket.
It pierced through everything I ever did,
my little sister's birthstar. She was my
favorite. She's been dead sixty years.
She died of whooping cough. And I turned out
to be an ordinary farmer. This star
in my back yard, this gravelly piece of ash
seems like, by rights, it should belong to me.

WOMAN PICKED UP BY UFO, FLOWN INTO BLACK HOLE

Hello, it's Lettie here. How're you doing, Wanette!
You saw my picture in the paper? I know.
My hair looks weird. It turned white.
The air in the black hole burned it, somehow.
Like getting a permanent when you're pregnant.
Well, I have trouble believing I'm alive,
so I figure who cares about the hair?

I'll tell you about it if you have the time.
I was just parking in the Acme lot,
twelve thirty on the worst day of my life.
The night before, Hank came home as mean
as a Tom Cat with his tail on fire.
His boss rides him. He drinks. When he comes home,
he slaps me around. He got me on the ear
and I could hear church bells all morning.

It took me down. For one thing, see, I love him.
I tried to leave Hank once, last summer.
You didn't know that? Well, I thought I'd go
this time for sure, right after I got him groceries.
I worked myself up, crying, missing him.
And that's when I got zapped. Outside the store
like a tornado—a black funnel cloud,
huge as the fist of God. It sucked me up.

Don't ask why, telling the story helps.
It's like putting something into the black hole.
Once you've been in, you have to find some way
to occupy yourself. Like knitting, the way
Betty always knits, but with my mouth.
I wait for folks to call. The piece in the paper's
got me a few calls. But they don't call twice.

No I didn't hear no voices, just this wind
like a monster vacuum cleaner coming down.
Some mouth organ sobbed the blues inside my head.
I never saw them. The story got it wrong.
Who could see anything? My whole head was
black as the high school auditorium
that day the movie stuttered, then stuck and tore
and Cooney couldn't find the right light switch.
Remember we got dizzy from the dark?

That's what a black hole is. Nothing. Nothing,
like I am without Hank. No job, no friends,
no self respect, like being turned inside out,
like disappearing, first one finger up to
the knuckle, then everything. Being eaten.
It felt like being skinned and boned and eaten.
This is personal, I know it is. Wanette!
Give me one minute. Wanette! Wanette?

SWEETHEARTS VANISH IN TUNNEL OF LOVE

You figured John and I wouldn't elope,
You wanted us to stay in your small town,
bound down and sensible. But love isn't
a tunnel, mother. It's a contraption
more like the human heart with chambers
you can climb around in—left ventricle,
right ventricle. If you set the ladder
squarely, you can ascend beyond yourself.
Before we meant to, we found ourselves looking
down where strings of streetlights defined
the little squares of shops and houses.
There was the bakery where Elsie pulled
the green awning down with a stick,
tugged her sweater around her and walked
home to seven children. The light
blinked out in Mr. Silver's jewelry shop.
Inside, the safe door swung shut on the ring
I would have worn. Now I don't need it,
mother. Can you see how tenderly
John and I look at one another, far up
and clarified, above the tiny world?
We look down at the stucco house we might
have lived in, and at you, mother, your face
no bigger than a number on my watch.
You are standing by the police sergeant
who says over and over "Just gone, just gone,"
like theme music to a commercial
you can't believe. But it's true,
it's true, we are finally alone together,
touching, each other's parents and each other's
children. And as for the future,
John has seen to that. He carried
our brown boat all the way on his back,
looking like a beautiful beetle,
in case we ever need to come back down.

HUMAN BOY FOUND IN INDIAN JUNGLE
AMONG WOLF PACK

He had apparently been nursed by a she wolf
and taught to hunt with the males.

For Derek Davis

I'll be your subject till the rainy season.
I stay in these white rooms because I want to.
But what you have taught me takes root in my brain.
Now I picture myself dressed and sitting
on your chair, talking. I like to push
my finger across the little insects you say
spell my name in your essays. I like
to see how the world is hardly any bigger
than a green melon and how one hand can make
it spin around. Now I believe the days
have names and that they live on a piece
of paper. Every night I practice loving
this blouse you gave me, which smells like a
human woman. But her smell quarrels
with the odor of my mother's stinging fur.
Inside my brain they fight like two cheetahs.

My mother taught me to run on all four legs.
I could follow the pack of silver fur
through the brushwood of the timberland,
flying after a fox like a ray of light
the moon had hurled into the stupid dark.

The snarling jungle vines were my veins.
I circled the bitter bark of the banyan tree
quiet as a python. My skin became
the nine different roughnesses of moss.
My joy was fluent as the underwater brooks.
Lying belly down on the steaming ferns
I could hear the scree of the small green bird,
almost out of range of human ears,
above the bellowing mountain waterfall.

It isn't grief, exactly, that I feel.
Doesn't grief finally loosen its claws,
fly off, and let its victim rest?
But this goes on and on. Beyond my wall
I see the amber streetlights burn like violent eyes
that want me again. I go out and howl,
but they never come. Tell me, is there
a time when it gets too late to go back?

MAN SURVIVES NINE DAYS IN RUBBLE
OF COLLAPSED BAKERY

Now, since Death walked into City Hall
in his black three piece suit and told the Mayor
that Irving Shiffman's been too much for him,
the people want to see me suddenly.

So why couldn't they take the plain word
of a baker who had flour on his nose,
who rose at four and put on clean underwear,
so they could buy fresh loaves before breakfast?
Did they need to have this building fall on me?
I should be a hero with a crushed chest,
so they could take my word when I scold them!
They bleat like telephones and race around.
They think that dying is fast as a computer.

But what's the use, teaching them to live?
Irving Shiffman's tongue is a poor mouse.
I'm a simple man who's learned a baker's patience.
If yeast spores live at all, they find breath slowly.
It's not worth mentioning that I've spent my days
waiting for colonies of living creatures
to awaken and stretch, to divide and divide again.
And the kneading—all that endless pounding
till my muscles can recite their own names.
Kneading makes the dough elastic to catch
the yeast's soul as it rises in the oven.

For nine days I lay dying in the darkness
beneath the rubble of a modern building.
I counted the fingers on my broken hand.
I thought of wheat and rye, slowly budding.
I rolled words from the Torah like pearl onions.
You want me to tell why I'm still here after
no food, no light, no water, nothing but pain
screaming like a siren for me to die
while they hacked and dug to find our broken bodies?
Irving Shiffman's soul hung back from death
because he'd practiced waiting. My soul sticks
to whistles and redbirds, to plain flour and water.
It hangs onto the world like rising yeast.

300 POUND WOMAN APPEARS TWO MONTHS
AFTER HER DEATH

They still haven't sold your house on Stubbs Street,
Edith. I walk here Saturdays, trying to recall you,
but I never thought I'd see you here like pale
greenish smoke beneath the porch light. If it's really
you, I wish you'd put the stars back where they were
before you died.
                           All my life I loved you.
You were a circus, come to town each day,
a big pink tent that God had pitched each summer,
size twenty-two in loud purple dresses,
with green dogs walking on your bust and hips.
When we were sick, you brought us scalloped beans.
When Lottie got gangrene, you watched her kids.
All summer you gave us tomatoes swelled like balloons.

Even in this town, people took notice.
They'd watch us clerking in the fabric store.
You'd measure yard goods, throw in polka dots,
give extra red away, call a sale on sleeves.
And your cotton with the stars was gone by noon—
girls saying "Oh, what luck!" and squeezing
their sacks to clamp the free stars in.

I went to school with half the girls who trade here—
Ellie from the Wash and Dry, Wanette and
the twins who clerk at Coast to Coast,
gossiped till they're thin and worked to the bone.
You were the only show in town, Edith,
and when you closed, I wanted to close with you.
The day we drove you to that graveyard
of brown grass fenced off from the soybean field,
everything—the beer, the songs—turned flat.

You're leading me somewhere. I'm put in mind of a breeze
curling up through crackling autumn leaves.
I see your old mums rattling in the cold,

You stir around them, trying to tell me something.
Your voice is like a wisp of garden fog.
"Look at this," you say, "start with this."
A puff of Queen Anne's lace, a constellation,
the white flowers racing together, clenching,
tightening, closing—I look where you point—
until I can see an actual star.

BLIND GENIUS DISCOVERS INFINITY

One morning tapping my cane from edge to edge
of the sidewalk, I found infinity. Before
I lost my sight, I'd studied math. Think of
the highest number—infinity is greater.

Impossible to think of then, but now
I find it lies between the edges of
the sidewalk, pure space, pure potential—
I could tap my cane down anywhere.

And mother has told me it's the same for her,
sitting beside the window watching me,
as she patiently untangles her yarn,
the two ends buried in the skein at first.

She undoes it, pulling out the knots
until there's everything to work with
like a long expectation deferred
from New Year's to next Christmas.

She's knitting a sweater for my father,
who has gone deer hunting this morning
with his cold rifle. The lunch she made—
deer meat and homemade bread—is buried in a pocket

of his rough jacket. He would take me
with him if I could see. He has told me
how all day long he crouches in his blind,
letting his desire fill up the woods,

thinking of the delicate foreheads, thinking
of the antlers just emerging. For him, waiting
must be like the immense space between the tap and
sharp tap of my cane, or like the sweater

spilling hugely from my mother's hands.
Can you imagine how my father, with a catch
in his throat, raises his gun then lowers it,
raises and lowers it again, uncertain in

the many-leaved fall afternoon because
he aches to see blood blooming on the flanks,
but he loves the deer so much he gives himself
only two shells. And all the space between.

MAN'S THUMB BLEEDS FOR THREE YEARS

I'm afraid they'll find out how I did it since
I can't stop the bleeding, but I've got an alibi
worked out—I sliced it skinning croaker.
If they believe that, they're dumber than I think,
cause a knife cuts clean and auto glass
breaks jagged and gives a ragged cut,
which is what I've got.

I came to work here at sixteen,
after my old man left. We install glass
in cars. It's quiet as a graveyard
since we all wear gloves, not to protect
our hands, to protect the glass. Outside,
around the parking lot, there's windows lined up
between wood stakes—
one city block of glass that can catch the sun
mornings and shine like water. At first
I liked putting windows into cars. Replacing
something smashed is better than serving
meat that turns to shit in hours.
Plus which, I thought I'd get some overtime,
enough to buy a keyboard. My old lady
said I could keep everything I made
over the rent. But bucks go fast and
overtime is scarcer than a good woman here,
so I have to practice on a keyboard I drew
on cardboard and it gets bloody.

What kept getting to me was the quiet,
like all those millions of car windows
resting on their sides between the stakes
was sheet after sheet of frozen sound.
I started to hate Manny, the guy who brought them in.
I'd see him unloading used ones from the truck
and I'd want to kill him for saving them from
the wrecker, like keeping their music locked
inside this thin shiny sheet. So I got a hammer,

cut the wire fence, and started smashing.
The night I let the music out
the sky was all bright riffs and chords
and now my head is clear, if only I
could do something about this bleeding thumb of mine.

III

LEAVING MY SON FOR THE FIRST TIME

For two years we'd breathed each other's breath.
When I was cold I stuffed you in your coat,
when I was hungry, I sliced an apple for you.
We were like two small townhouses
looking into one another's windows

along the streets of Philadelphia
where the bricks bond like
family secrets, where tourists warm
themselves with someone else's history.
Your history was my history

until I had to leave for London,
to walk its space into my feet,
streets so wide the buildings didn't know
each other's names. Here I am myself.
Every heart, armed with stubborn architecture.

Every night I come to this hotel room
with two formal beds, where rain
and darkness beat their broken wings
against the window, trying to get in
and I wonder every night

how the windows turn everything away.
And yet these streets begin to seem my streets.
Listen, son, London must be a name
for the place I can invent myself—and you,
drinking your own milk, back home.

LONDON UNDERGROUND

Sitting in my hotel room
leaning forward like a blind woman
I can hear the rumble under ground
shaking the floor—the landslide
which has always been going on beneath the world,
like the great human heart breaking over
and over, fearing something worse.

I can follow its sadness all the way
from Holborn to King's Cross,
from Lancaster Gate to Chancery Lane
and back, a train swishing through arches
whose ribs are clogged with
a hundred years of soot.
But didn't the Guide Book say
the Underground has also been a refuge?
It held a thousand cribs in 1942,
orphans whose lives deceived the bombs.

What if one of those orphans
grew up to be the woman
who sold you a bright scarf
today on Portobello Road, laughing,
touching your shoulder
in the hazy London sunlight?

AMERICAN TOURIST AT COVENT GARDEN

When I woke one morning in my hotel in London,
I was already imagining not being here.
I was a cracked cistern. England was trickling away.

I mourned for what I hadn't even lost.
Crazy with longing, I picked up my Guide Book.
It told me to go to Covent Garden

where Lisa Doolittle found her real London.
A queen's language bubbled in her mouth.
The dirt around her neck turned into golden beads.

So I took the bus to Covent Garden.
What I found there was the old longing—
a sad faced man whose bulldog barked like a loose cough,

teenagers leaning against one another like praying hands,
the laundromat mistress with the figure of a child,
and a lot of pigeons trying to be friends.

I wanted anything that lasted. I wanted
to trade fleeting London for one cheap postcard.
I wanted to pick up pebbles and cram my heart with them.

But in the middle of the square a young girl
with hair like puffs of gold smoke played the cello.
Mozart, who ended in a pauper's grave.

It's all right, the music said. You must be empty
so London can pour through you forever
like water flashing through a tile culvert.

I held still and let the music flash through me.
When the girl passed the hat, I gave and gave.

PADDINGTON STATION AT MIDNIGHT

Notice: Underground trains running
from this station stop at 11:45 p.m.

After the last train full of people had slid out, after
the last noisy food bar had been padlocked,

after the last garrulous trainman
had bowlegged his dark way home

and under the huge arches nothing talked
but cold and emptiness, that's when the station

started its work, erasing us. Then the steel beams
stared at us through empty rivet holes,

then shadows tried to stick to our hands and faces,
then I heard the sound was dwindling from our voices

and I knew that if we took another step, it would be
into nothing. But then the newspapers pulled in,

filling whole cars of lumbering night trains.
They had made their way through terrible distances—

a message sent from brain to eyes,
to the shaking fingers, to the fast machines—

they could have snagged and crumpled any time.
But bundles of them flew onto the platform

where they lay ordered as stacks of linen napkins,
every headline resolving itself to speak

against the terrible silence, against all odds.

COLD WAR

> As road and rail freeze worsens all over Europe,
> England awaits the terrible cold.
> January 10, *London Evening Standard*

In Moscow the temperature has fallen so low,
a man stepped out to go to work
and his heart exploded. Another's nose froze solid.
A third lost his cheeks. Cold is moving
across Europe, East to West, like an eyelid
closing over hope, like a hawk's shadow
shutting off the sun.

This cold is deadlier than stone.
But it will only kill the ones it frightens.
It won't help to be afraid.
Untense your shoulders. Unclench your fists.
Try to trust your body.

Outside Parliament the statue of Winston Churchill
embraces the difficult weather.
In Trafalgar Square snow settles
on Lord Nelson's eyebrows like transforming wisdom.
Even men you cannot recognize,
who in the past seemed unremarkable,
leap onto the train, shaking snow
like splendid wings that flare from their black coats.

Open your eyes. Look up.
Try to see beyond the Thames,
beyond the way the pale lights stain the water.
Try to see beyond the silent graves
of Thomas More and Karl Marx.
Look beyond the great dome of St. Paul's.

Maybe London will arise in white,
the triumphant city, like a shy bride
finally stepping out of her stone clothes.

DRIVING BY WESTMINSTER ABBEY
AFTER MIDNIGHT

Why are the lights on late in the cathedral?
The kings and queens cannot be settling their accounts.
Fame has cancelled everything they owed.
They can't be eating. They can't be dancing.

Long ago, coming to their stories' end,
they lay down by one another in their crypts,
wearing to the end their favorite hats, peculiar shoes.
They fit their heads to the delicate pillows,
settled their hands on their chests
like hinged oyster shells, to pray,
settled their legs into a position they could enjoy
for a hundred thousand years, closed their eyes,
and began to practice silence.

This is why the lights are on so late in Westminster Abbey.
The maid is dusting the kings and queens,
laughing gently at this one and that—
the queen who took her mangy stoat to bed with her,
the king who had a hunchback he tried to hide,
and the Prince whose five o'clock shadow
stretched over Europe like a small Dark Ages.

Around them the maid's feather duster
whispers fondly, hitting granite sometimes
like the clink of a marimba.

THEATER

Away from front desks in hotels they slip,
out of restaurants they lurch, untying
their aprons, unpinning their hair nets,
powdering their noses, pulling on silk shirts.

From the cash registers of clothing stores
they come, and out of factories they wake
like the dead who have heard a trumpet,
who rise and hurry through the narrow alleys,

this one already pursing her full lips
into the pout of a mean grimace,
that one screwing his peg leg in place,
the other shaking her hanky into a full blown rose.

Down the streets and sidewalks they pour
like rain, intent, clarified, and splendid,
pulling on their golden, high-heeled slippers,
learning how to juggle as they run,

because every one of them has been called back—
no one has been cut—there are enough parts,
and as dusk is falling, one by one
they converge upon the Stage Door, and are let in.

CUTPURSE

If I had stopped in a rush of deep love and spent
the money on that blouse as red as the blush
that rises after a full kiss on the mouth,

or if I had dropped the bills like seeds
into the dirty pocket of that drunk
who begged on the sidewalk, or if I had only snapped

my shoelace, so I'd had to leave
ten mortal minutes later, I might not have felt
the strap slip off, the purse go light and vanish.

When it was gone, I didn't have a shilling for the bus,
no driver's license, no passport,
nothing to hold me down to earth.

I felt bodiless and nameless in the clash
of evening traffic. Above me, some monumental clock
clanged five across the city and

I looked up into the face of time, who someday
will take my skin, my flesh, my bones
until I stand empty as pure hunger,

transparent as clean glass in sunlight—
while the bell pealed and pealed, a sound like
joy that in my life I never earned or paid for.

FLYING HOME

It's Sunday morning in the London airport.
I'm leaving for home. Through the serious windows
the sky pours everything it knows—
weak light drooling through fog.

It's like looking through scratched glasses,
like wearing a thin bandage on my eyes.
Yesterday sun glinted between the brick buildings
as though it were a dozen spangled earrings

or a gust of yellow papers blown
carelessly beneath our feet.
The sun was a gypsy in yellow scarves, her fingers
sassing back the fog with silver bells.

But today the runway isn't visible.
I only want to deceive the fog, get off the ground,
to sit above the wings, feeling the frail
miraculous airplane slice the sullen sky

like lightning, like my grandmother's
brilliant needle slipping through gray flannel,
the way, after all these years,
I walk in our door at dusk

and children's laughter rings through the house
stitching everything together.

IV

INSPECTING THE GARDEN AFTER DARK

A few things I know: I know that you're my son.
This back yard is your home, and you are
crawling on fat knees over this mound
of black dirt, dragging your diaper the way the night
is dragging a wet moon into the sky.
You can say *mama* and *daddy*. But you whisper
mama to onions and *daddy* to the asters.
I've already lost you. Or maybe never had you,
safe in your crib with blankets by the night light.
The asters know your kiss. It's wet as a slug's.
What do you have to do with these morning glories,
unpacking leaves, hundreds of them escaping
with umbrellas, holding their homes in their own hearts?
See how the cabbage patiently folds one day
after another over his secret name?
If I could, I'd peel your days away like leaves
and finally find the name that's yours.
I think back, December, May, leaf by leaf
to last year at this time, when your heart
was a wish in God's mouth beating to get out.

COMING INTO HISTORY

While I sit in south light, suspecting nothing,
your cells begin to read the hidden code
which teaches your hand it must become the hand
and informs the foot of its own metatarsal.
Every minute, now, is hazardous.
Suppose your cells forget their language?
Suppose the language they know is monstrous?
But your tiny body lengthens, becomes a stalk.
The vertebrae bubble on your spine like pearls.
Your head begins to bulge. Your eyes appear
like flecks of pepper. Your nervous system spreads
its net. And then in the fourth week, your heart
starts beating. Careful and adroit, your cells
rehearse, trying to crowd out accident,
filling up the acquiescent water.
They copy their nature over and over like doom,
straining to make alternatives unthinkable,
practicing to grow inevitable,
to bring your body into history where
the midwife's hands are drawing on their gloves.

NAMING YOU

Today we named you for our dead fathers,
Edwin Daniel, son of an Irish bricklayer,
and John Gerald, son of a Swedish shopkeeper.
We've learned you are a boy. Wanting to see
something about you besides your ghoulish bones
which glowed on ultra-sound two months ago,
we stood in the kitchen tonight, eyes clouded
by fragrant steam, and uttered name after name
to find you. Michael. Samuel.
Noah. Nebuchadnezzer. It could be
anything, the way we ourselves could have been
anything. If any other boat had touched the shore—
If our fathers had never met the women they married—
If your father had never called me to have tea
that April day in 1975—If I had not said yes,
your name could be anything. But I said yes.
We had tea. Our fathers met their wives.
No other boat touched any other shore and you
are you. And so we wrote in indelible ink
the names your bones already bear, John Edwin Daniel Larkin.

READING *THE NEW YORK TIMES*

You flutter for your life inside my belly,
swimming the quick stroke of the unborn
and I look up from making the morning toast,
reading the New York Times. I feel your splash
like the shiver of a tambourine
above the paper's cool, factual voice.
It numbers buried silos in North Dakota.
And today I can imagine them being fired.
First strike capability.
Equal to so many tons of TNT.
You flutter. The paper calculates how many
times each human being could die and this time
you must be counted. Our skin would sag like rotting
cloth, our eyebrows singe and crumble,
our faces be undressed to skulls together.
Above this voice reciting death
you bang your tambourine to tell me you are
growing eyes and toes. You're a parade.
You strike up the band and kick high for dear life.

SLEEP

I've read that in pregnancy the brain sends out
a stupefying drug. No wonder I gather sleep
like cotton, fist over fist, cramming
some blurring bag until I barely know
whose life I stand in. Could this slowing
of the senses have been passed by some mother
to her daughters several thousand years ago
to muffle the noise of grief, to save
the young for love or for the chance of love?
So you can't hear women rolling dice
for bread, talking with the bones of their
dead children. So you can't see
the lost face of a baby, born on time
and strong, but born in the wrong place,
who had to be put to bed in earth at noon
while his mother watched, her eyes bloodshot
as the unblinking sky where red dust rises.
To keep you safe for love. So you won't feel
too soon the hunger which no crop on earth
can touch, I turn and harvest sleep.

THINKING ABOUT MY OWN DEATH

Listen. You aren't even born and already
I open our front door to firethorn shooting
in sun, to the jazz of swift traffic
on thirty-fourth and think, what if I die
and leave you? Half the time I can't
imagine any future once you get here.
The other half I imagine lying in the sleazy
hands of death while you toddle near a
fast radial tire. My imagination's like a bus
going west beyond North Platte, Nebraska,
stranding us both in the last station
where the white-faced agent's deaf and dumb.
Women do still die in childbirth. Children
still shrink in corners under the frugal gaze
of stepmothers. It could happen to you.
And how to leave directions to someone else?
I stand in the lavish afternoon light
wanting to write what music to use hollering
hello to you when you run home, directions
for exactly how to touch your face.

OVERDUE

If your great grandmother could
put her old lips to my stomach,
she'd tell you to be born,
get started. *It won't work
to hang back,* she'd mutter. *Sooner
or later you have to pick the beans,
paint all the buildings.*

She'd whisper this advice if
she weren't far away, on her day bed
where the milky shades are drawn,
surrendering her sight
of the huge daisy in the wallpaper
and the ordinary way
she used to find the bathroom.

The more she gives away,
the less she worries. She has already
forgotten her right hand, mislaid
the farms she sowed and reaped,
the crops she haggled over
in the market like a man
then finally sold, saying

Take your licking early, and get out.
Now she's following her own advice.
She sleeps whole crops away,
time running through her faster
than sand through an hourglass,
her brown legs propped in carpet slippers,
her nose tearing the air in little whistles,

while snowfalls shake
the Minnesota sky inside out,
while all around her Johnsons

and Baumans buy and sell the land.
She's getting out of town
and she hasn't even met you.

You are her last great grandson,
tag end, tardy to take your place.
But you might still meet her,
she might still hold you in her stiffening arms
and mutter a blessing on you
if you will take your licking early
and get out.

INVOCATION TO A BABY ALREADY
TWELVE DAYS OVERDUE

It's May. This is the month wild with choices.
You can rush into the strolling sunshine
to join forsythia bursting like popcorn,
and weeping cherry, and the woodthrush whose song
pulsed in southlight this morning.

Come with your hands open or shut.
Come with them slippery from blood.
Don't be afraid. Only slide down a cascade of water.
Come with you eyes azure as pieces of sky.
Or come with eyes a dark complication of gray.

Come trailing the left-over placenta.
Come with vernix like wax over pale new cheese.
Come with no clothes but the color rose
which quickens your flesh.
Come skinny or fat.

Come with hair black as a grand piano,
shouting in fifteen keys together or
come with a throat as calm
as the throat of a beautiful vase.
The world will fill you with sound.

Come out from where you are hiding.
The count is up now, the game is over.
Come home to this small room.
You'll be as free and as bound
as the star that's framed tonight

in the window above your empty crib.

HOW LABOR STARTS

I lie under one clean white sheet
beside your father.
We are hardly breathing.
Through the formal window
a northwest wind drifts down,
perhaps from Minnesota,
disordering the curtains,
suggesting things in the dark:
wet docks, lizards, lost shoes,
flotsam of childhood
wafting across the mind,
nothing in particular
but still not nothing.
And then a sound
like the whisper of a boat
pulling in at Hallin's dock.
From a wide lake
where incandescent water folds
over and over itself,
the boat arrives
through the fragrance
of decaying seaweeds,
and in the precise moment
it brushes the wooden pilings
oh, something, something
starts way back in the bloodstream
like the faintest trickle
of pitocin invading
this wide night
and I get up
clutching my cotton bathrobe,
thinking
a stranger must be riding
this small boat.
Tomorrow must be here,

you must be lighting now.
Across the cerebral cortex,
across the deep median sagittal groove,
across the corpus callosum
a contraction
comes.

BIRTH

I watch the midwife pull the white paper down.
She rips the old part off, pats the table,
says "Climb up here. Use the stirrups."

Granite shifts along a fault, striking sparks.
"Is this comfortable?" she asks.
I gasp and breathe, hout, hout hout,

while she unpacks chrome instruments.
She tilts the spotlight down,
trains its glare to the perineum.

The contraction grinds our muscles
on each other, tearing continents apart.
your skull scrapes my backbone till

lightning torches all our ribs.
I search the earth for a way out of this.
But we are the earth. The earth fractures itself.

"Relax," the midwife says in another language.
The membrane breaks, weeping light and water.
You ride water downstream, towards the falls and

"Push!" she says. Light pours over the edge,
floods the table, stuns the midwife's
knotty hands. In one minute,

a new order, a new earth, transforming
old orthodoxies, transfiguring the room.
In the end, we are faithful

to what cannot be avoided.
Light breaks from your new knees
and shoulders. Light peals
like an unbearable, high bell.

SHIRT

When they unbraided you,
long curving muscle,
from my body
and laid you on my stomach
to breathe your own way
still smelling like my blood
I tried to stop my shaking,
to lie still as earth
so you could burrow,

your warm snout nudging
my breast until
the nurse took you from me,
washed you and pulled
the shirt over your head.
When she gave you back
to me, your face
clean, your shirt
and diaper white,
you were a citizen.

VITAL SIGNS AT MIDNIGHT

After your birth I lie in this hard bed
all day, trying to get the habit of your new body
until the sun sinks down, pulling radiance
after it. Down the long slope into night

we slide away from your brilliant birth
until the night nurse comes to take our vital
signs and snaps the light off. Helpless then,
I go on squinting at your outline—

your neat head, your ears like rosemoles,
your drawn up legs, your breathing a moist snuffle.
By midnight we are more strange
to one another than two lost children.

We lie together in the hemorrhaging darkness
sharing blood and fever, all our functions leaking,
draining back to where birth meets death
and I feel that I am swimming for our lives

on the black underside of a dark pit, my muscles
slack with your weakness, my breast a bruise
where your mouth sucks, your small feet
fluttering against my wounded uterus,

and I try to be mother to us both, carefully
holding you, a stranger, in my hands while I struggle
up through the black canal of terrible water,
through birthrings of dark pain

to gather you towards home.

RECOVERING THE COMMONPLACE

for Bob Perkel

No wonder your juice turned sour.
No wonder the long night rolled up like a mat.
No wonder light returned so furtively
we guessed it mislaid something.

When we woke up
you were too hot to say *mama.*
I lifted you from your crib.
But you were too sick to pee.

When we drove you to the doctor,
rain was falling. No wonder. This is
the way things happen.
In the waiting room, I prayed

the ordinary blue chairs
be places no one's child
could die, had ever died.
Then far away in your eye a light

stirred. *Cup, table,* and everything
recalled itself. You uncurled and cried
"Cracker!" "Apple Juice!"
Slowly, like sunrise practicing again

to make another morning, you sat up.
The doctor let you listen
to your heart. He held
his tiny light up to your finger.

It glowed truthful, red. By this time
you had given back your fever
like a toy you'd played with long enough.
You lay on the table baring your face,

your whole naked chest and penis.
When you peed high into the air
the room was all clarity and dazzle,
as though it were the simplest thing.

JUST TO WARN YOU

There's a suicide in the house and you're it,
pulling your screams out bright as knives to show us
what you've got to take us down with
if we stop you. We can have things your way
or not at all. And either way is deadly.
You hurl yourself, shrieking, down the stairs.
You pull dogs' tails, clog your throat with tissue,
and choking, grope for matches. When I interfere
to save you, you stick your lip out like a platter.

Listen child, I want to make peace, early,
all around. Fire, gravity—
I don't control these things. I only learned
them recently myself. You make a treaty with them
or you die. I mean to keep you safe
against the world; one day you may find tender
uses for it.
                    Someday when you are walking into
the sun, your heart may lose its footing. You may plunge
from your high wire, no net beneath, to love.
Then you'll praise gravity, which, stubborn still,
might balance you on earth.

MAKING PEACE

Sitting on the floor in your plaid shirt,
you cry and beat the air with a broomstraw.
Your heart is breaking because you hear
my voice lunging at you whenever you sneak
back to the wreck of philodendron by the window.
Already you have strangled the plant's throat.

"The plants were here before we were," I say.
You stop crying to look at me, your eyes hooded
in love and misery. You are a soldier,
tearing the fingers from the enemy.
Next you crawl away to find the sun. You want
to hide it in your pocket. I bring out

your yellow ball and roll it to you.
Back and forth we roll the sun, from you to me,
back and forth, extinguishing tomorrow's wars with light.
Today your skin's the texture of those roses
that bloom apricot all summer, and your
light brown hair is finally coming in, pinwheeling

like another galaxy, just born.

LOOKING AT A PICTURE THAT HASN'T
BEEN TAKEN YET

You're running in morning light. Your stomach's
pouched out, you're squealing. It's an ordinary day,
perhaps in summer when your mind is flexing,
springing towards a thought the way a cat
leaps safely, tree to tree.

In the house next door a pale boy is watching,
his gun propped through an open window.
Above, clouds are unrolling, slow as history.
The ramshackle house is settling dangerously.
Wind's standing still. The dark stairs are ticking.

The boy, casual as death, watches you
while you spring like a cat—volitional, weightless,
giving your body gladly to the air,
thinking *it's summer, I'm alive, I'm here,*
and then the thought stops you   *But I'm going
to die.*
Death lays the weapon on the window sill
watching the rich blood pumping from your side.
By the time you read this, you'll know the wound I mean.

DRIVING HOME IN THE BLIZZARD

I wade to the North lot, through snow so weightless
the breath of one sparrow could make it drift
and I find my Volkswagen changed to a blank
hump. I scrape the windshield, bare the good

familiar flanks, recarve the nimble lines,
create the shape I need for getting home.
I climb into its safe, dark cave
turn the key, and snap the radio on:

there snow is blurring Bach's Brandenberg
Concerto. The car floats sideways into
traffic and I remember moving sideways
into anything that ever mattered.

As I pull up at the stoplight on
College Avenue, I hear they've closed toy
stores, dentists' offices. Childbirth classes,
canceled. Holy Spirit Prep called off at

noon. Bus 19 to be delayed by hours.
All the way to Philadelphia I see
lights going out, doors locking, and finally
J. S. Bach is closing down so the D. J. can

say which other voices will be muffled
when I get home. I snap the radio off.
Snow teems and touches everything until
each separate shape is drawn to every other

until the air is one woven garment
of truth, lighting and lighting everything.
And while the patient Volkswagen idles
on the bridge beside the auto graveyard,

it's not so bad that those firm shapes
are crumbling to rust under a rug of snow.
Such deep silence makes you want to throw your
voice beyond the row of cars, beyond the

streets where the mailbox is muffled and
the stop sign grows new wisdom like a beard.
I am listening to snow's final silence linger
in the darkening afternoon, thinking how

once home, I will call everyone I know
to say *it's not so bad, it's not so bad.*

POEM TO SAY TO A CHILD WHILE FOLDING
HIS OUTGROWN CLOTHING

While you were still unborn
our friends brought, one by one,
the clothes their children had worn:
shirts with secret pockets,
blankets, a tie gown.

And because we were unable
to find you anywhere
we pulled you from the pockets,
we stitched a fable
of a baby yet unborn.

When you finally came
we dressed you in those clothes.
All winter they were kind.
Now I fold the clothes away,
a legacy refined.
Someone else's child
may briefly take his turn.

For parents, now, who wait,
imagining new faces,
I will enumerate
the children whose graces
became your warmest jacket:

Elizabeth and Melissa,
Patrick, Andrew, Kate
wore these clothes once.
Teddy, Bess, and Ethan.
And may their loveliness
wherever these clothes are worn
shield against loss
and pass to those unborn.

DANCING IN EARLY EVENING

Your daddy heads home, driving
through the old routine
of Fall, following
the protocol of
yellow lines.
Two feet's mistake
in any direction,
death. He stays on
track, bound down, so
far, so good.

At the Spring Garden exit
your daddy points his
blue Toyota
toward your crib.
The band tunes up. As
though you heard him, you
throw out your arms, scribbling
grace notes in the air,
head bobbing.
He walks in the door and

snatches you to winch
you up, he heaves
you to a swandive and
you exchange love talk.
You lay your bald head on
his worsted shoulder,
woo him with contralto
toots and drooling.
Then the two of you step out
together, polishing
the floor, your diaper

bagging, pooching, your
fuzzy blue socks flashing, as
night descends, the two
of you untying
obsolete routines, unloosening
gravity's old malice,
holding one another in
the lamplight, shooby,
romping, dancing, rising,
floating clear of death.
Yeah. Oh yeah.